Cotton Candies

A Collection of Poems

Bea,

Your support
means a lot!
Thank you
so much!
I hope you
like it. ♡

JOWIE ESPIRITU
The Write Rhythm

Cotton Candies

Printed in the United States of America

ISBN: 9798842659449

Sunrise

Dawn

A new dawn smiles on the waking east,
Bringing hope to the earth's fair slumber;
The dawn may think it's required, at least,
To loom with care in distant amber.

A streak of light commences the day,
Breaking the cold of the night before;
Prepared to defer its warmth away,
As if it's what the earth does implore.

A new day begins, hope it begets,
Seize it we must, a gift from above;
No more should we grieve, no more regrets,
New hope to dwell in the Father's love.

Here Comes the Morning

Step outside for a new day has come,
Here comes the morning!
The sun that wakes the world with light
Has broken the darkness and casts out the night.
Here comes the morning!

Feel the breeze so cool and fresh,
Here comes the morning!
The dewdrops that fell on the face of the earth
Will nourish the ground and to seeds give birth.
Here comes the morning!

See the beauty the sunshine brings,
Here comes the morning!
The colors that burst with life in nature
Has wakened the land and all God's creatures.
Here comes the morning!

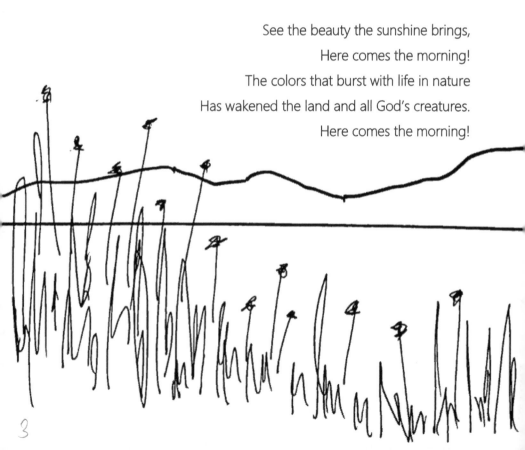

Hear the songs the birds go singing,
Here comes the morning!
The tunes they sing that fill the air
Bring music to the heart, no burden to bear.
Here comes the morning!

Praise You, Lord, for everything You made,
You made the morning!
The world we enjoy, the world where we stay
Comes from Your bounty and so do we say,
Praise God for the morning!

Mornings

Mornings are a reminder
     that it is okay to start again.

Life is not always filled
     with the sweetness of victory.
Sometimes, we may taste
     the bitterness of defeat.

But just like the morning—
     rising again after a long night,
     we must not cease
     from trying again and again,
     we must learn
     to stand up on our feet
     even after how many times
     we fall.

5

Each morning
is a chance to
BEGIN ANEW
and an opportunity
to keep moving
forward.

Shortcuts

There are no shortcuts in life.
Even the sun takes time to shine.

Do not be in a hurry.

Whether you are
in the highest point of life,
take time to savor the moment,

or even when you are
in the most painful
time of your life,
let it teach you
to be still
as you wait for the time
it will be over.

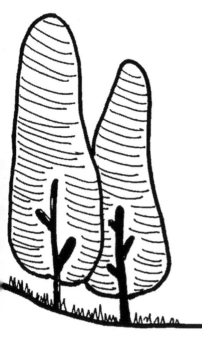

Morning Bliss

in the morning mist
    at the start of day,
when the sun has kissed
    the night away,
is there a better moment—
    a moment like this—
to commune with God,
    what joy, what bliss!

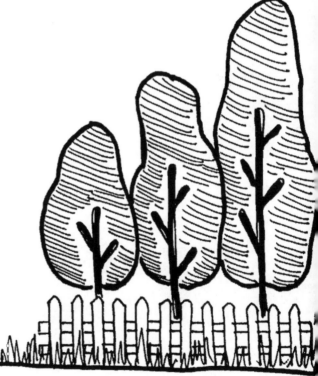

Eastern Skies

And when the glorious light
comes beaming on the east,
it casted all the darkness
the previous night released;
and in that tender dawning
of the light on eastern skies,
comes all of heaven's graces
to bless us when we rise.

The best
mornings
are enjoyed
OUTSIDE
so get up,
go out,
and enjoy
your day.

NO

lifted

The fog is lifted
>   morning after morning
>   to remind us
>   that God's love
>   is eternal.

The morning
comes to whisper
HOPE
that we will
rise again
after we
fall.

Mood

May your mood
    rise up as the morning
    and stay the same
    'til the fall of night.
May your life
    be filled with joy today
    and stay the same
    as the morning bright.

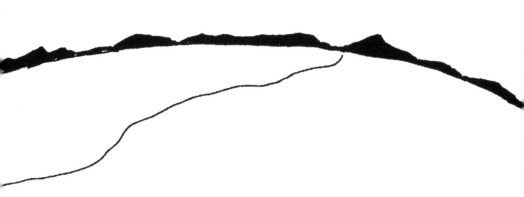

Rise

Always remember
    that the number
    of times
    the sun will set
    is also the number
    of times
    it will rise.

So don't lose hope.

14

Dawning Sun

The brightness of the dawning sun
gleaming over the horizon
bears the promise of new strength,
and as we rise to face
the new challenges
that confronts us each day,
we know we shall overcome.

Always
keep your face
towards the
SUNSHINE
and shadows
will fall
behind you.

17

Mountains

Worth It

Keep climbing your mountain.
   Every step
   may not be easy,
   but when you get
   to the top,
   every step will be
   worth it.

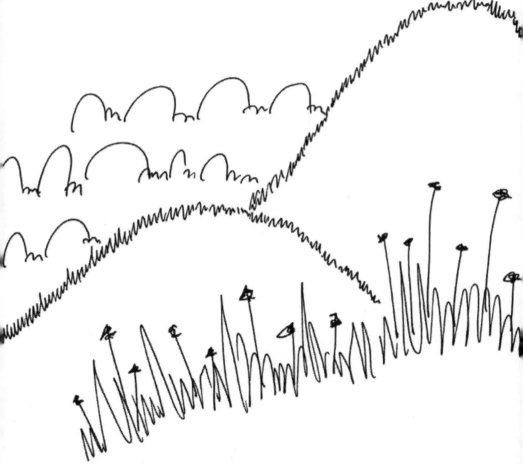

Too High to Climb

A mountain
is only too high to climb
if you climb it
all at once.

Climb it
one step at a time
and you will see
that there is no mountain
that cannot be
conquered.

An Uphill Climb

When life feels
    like an uphill climb,
    just remember
    that though mountains
    can cast shadows
    over the valleys,
    no mountain
    can ever block
    the sun.

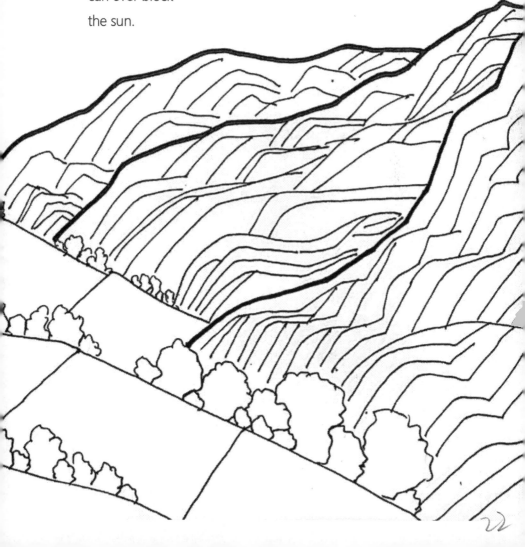

The best way
to conquer a
MOUNTAIN
is to conquer it
one step at
a time.

Mountain Top

Have you ever wished
to stand on a mountain top,
whisper all your worries to the wind,
tell yourself that it is okay to cry—
for tears are a way for you
to see the world
more clearly?

Climbing

Sometimes,
climbing your hardest mountains
is the only way to see
the greatest views
life can offer.

A Million Times Over

You may climb a mountain
a million times, and say,
you have conquered it
a million times over,
but never even once
it will bow down
to you.

26

Clouds

Cotton Candies

Soft as cotton candies
hanging from the heavens
on a windy summer day
when the sun stays high
and the field is clothed
in a vast verdant veil of silk
dotted by flowers fair and wild
among the graceful sway
of the slender blades of grass
like waves of oceans green
where tiny bees hover around
and birds feast the ground,
I gazed up to the lofty sky
and clouds passed me by.

Behind the Clouds

Behind the clouds
      that made the rain,
there hides the sun
      still shining bright—
for no amount
      of rain or clouds
could change the fact
      that it still shines.

Daydreaming

I would ride the clouds
And rush through the heavens
The wind is in my command

I will sail above the earth
In the speed of the angels
Trailing like a shooting star

In my dreams I can do anything
All power is mine
In space and time

Until awakened.
Until awakened.

Control

Don't force things to go your way.
Even rivers cannot control
which way the water goes
when it floods.
Even the clouds cannot dictate
which direction they should go
when the wind blows.

33

Value Each Day

A gloomy day teaches us
    to value the sun.
A sunny day teaches us
    to value the rain.
Life is sometimes sunny or gloomy,
    and we must learn
    to value each day.

Start Again

when you begin to feel
like life is a constant turns
of rising and falling
and of happiness and pain,
think again and realize
that every evening
is a chance to rest, and
every morning is a chance
to start again.

Try to look
at the world
from a different
PERSPECTIVE
so that you will
better understand
its wonders.

We Will Never Know

We will never know

      how much time we have left to live

      and see the beauty of the morning sun,

      taste the sweetness of the falling rain,

      smell the scent of the flowers blooming,

      feel the silence of the peaceful night,

      or hear the whisper of the gentle breeze.

And before we run out of time,

      we must make it our goal

      to live every moment

      as if it was our last.

It's not always SUNSHINES and RAINBOWS but the sun shall rise again tomorrow.

Kite

The way we see it,

    when we lose hold of the string,

    the kite is lost.

But for the kite,

    it is actually,

    at last,

    free.

Fields

41

Take Time

Take time to appreciate
    the glory of the sun rising,
    the fragrance of the flowers blooming,
    the melody of the birds singing,
    the freshness of the rain falling,
    and maybe then,
    just maybe,
    you'll truly find beauty
    and happiness
    among the chaos
    and sadness
    in your life.

I hope
all your tears
will be able
to water the

FLOWERBEDS

you are trying
to grow.

JB

Other People's Gardens

No matter how beautiful
    the flowers we can grow,
    we can't force
    to plant them
    on other people's
    gardens.

Dandelion's Charm

You will find me—

in the dandelion's charm
as it sways in the wind
and dazzles in the sun
when the spring has come
and it's finally warm.

You will find me—

when you look
with your eyes closed
and your senses open
to the whispers of the breeze
and the giggles of the blades.

You will find me—

for a moment,
finally happy
and free.

45

The Colors She Wears

A lovely butterfly
    gliding through the fields
    of fragrant flowers dainty
    against the vibrant leaves
    bathed by the sun
    on a cloudy day,
Has caught my eyes
    and whispered to my soul
    that she did not choose
    the colors she wears
    but she is thankful
    that she was given
    a love pair of wings.

Different Grounds

All of us are seeds
    planted on different grounds.
Wherever we are planted,
    we all have the choice—

    to bloom
    or die.

Seeds

every little seed you have
    make sure you sow,
whatever you sow today
    you will reap tomorrow;
growing those seeds
    may sometimes seem slow,
but from all those seeds
    good fruits will grow.

Fertile Ground

Your heart
is like a fertile ground.
Whatever you plant
shall definitely grow.
Choose your seeds
ever wisely.

49

Dance

I watched them dance
      through the newly-dried earth
      in a frantic rhythm
      and a cryptic song
      that echoed in my soul.
Their mighty wings
      cloaked over their backs
      as props and costumes
      they mastered to use
      to gracefully move
      in the gentle wind.
And I, inspired
      and slowly entranced
      by the soul-searing sound
      and the breath-taking pound
      have started to sway
      in the black birds'
      eternal dance.

A flower
that blooms in the
HARSHEST
WEATHER
is always the
best flower
of all.

Grass

Sad is the grass,
untouched by the sun,
unshaken by the wind
on a gloomy summer's day
when the cloud-covered sky
hides the sun away,
and the breeze unfelt,
freezes the flower fields
that once swayed with joy
and made me smile
but now made me smile
no more.

Birds Haiku

Birds on the treetops
singing merrily their song;
what joy to hear them.

On a lovely day
when the sky is clear and blue,
I hear them singing.

What music they bring
to my ears and to my soul!
What lovely creatures!

But then the weather—
all of a sudden has changed;
the clouds have gathered.

What power have they
to stop the clouds from forming?
Power they have none.

And so went silent
the poor birds on the treetops,
and their song was gone.

Rain

Mighty Rain

The mighty rain poured today
      like never in a thousand years,
It flooded my heart, my soul, my world—
      this rain has poured as did my tears;
If I could stop this rain from raging,
      how would the thirsty ground respond?
And if this rain would heal my aching,
      would it soothe the pain beyond?

58

What do you do
WHEN IT RAINS
in the middle of
a good day
but to wait
for the rain
to pass?

A Passing Rain

A sweet lullaby
    was sung by the rain
    on the roof, on the grass,
    in the wind, in the splash.
It knocked on my window pane
    and it washed the walls
    of my heart like tears
    for the wasted years
    and unnecessary pain.
And when it was done,
    it was then all gone,
    just as it was—
    a passing rain.

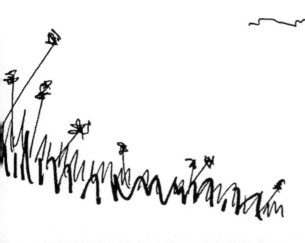

You can't
stop the rain.
Learn to
DANCE
in it when
it falls.

In Your Life

It may be raining so hard
in your life today,
it will pass.
You will see the sun
tomorrow.

62

You can
never stop
the RAIN
but you can
enjoy it.

Dark, Rainy Days

the dark,
rainy days
make us
appreciate more
the bright,
sunny ones.

64

As long
as there is life,
THERE is HOPE
even after the
storm.

Seasons

Seasons

In every changing season,
     however the change may be,
     we simply just adapt.

     That's the way it is.

Snow

Just like the snow,
he is free and fragile,
falling on the ground,
blown by the chill,
so perfect but so cold,
a wonder to behold.
But what really is snow?
Nothing, oh nothing—
it lives through the winter,
it leaves in the spring.

Cold

Even the warmth
of the shining sun
doesn't seem to have
any power to thaw
the ever cold snow
and melt it
into rivers of tears
that flow
from my ever cold
and lonely heart.

Spring

Buds start shooting
      from the wet ground
      sprinkled by the
      soft, sweet rain.
The tiny leaves
      gently touched
      by the fresh April wind
      and just like them,
      I started to comprehend
      that cold and lonely winters
      are not forever.

Everything has become
      new again
      in spring.

Thunderstorm

Flashes of yellow electric light
from the wide open vanilla skies
crackling down to the ground
with a mighty drumming sound,
terrifying, electrifying, energy bolting
through the ash gray clouds
gathering up in the distance
and the rain falling in an instance
filling up the little puddles
and the wind howling louder and louder
blowing colder and colder
bringing a cuddle weather
while I, thankfully safe and warm,
watched the summer thunderstorm
through my window.

Summer

The days are long
and the days are bright
as the earth is tilted
towards the sun
and the days are warm
and kids now run
out in the heat
playing barefoot
on the newly-mowed
lawn so neat
and the kid in me
wants nothing more
than to run outside
and once again
be young and free.

Fall

The leaves have started
to wither and die
and they turned pink or yellow, orange or red
and they will fall on to the grassy bed
and in a blink of an eye a cold blanket of white
will once again cover all the ground
it will be the end of all the happiness
I felt in my heart
and then just like the leaves,
I will fall to ground
and I will wait for the time
I will come out
alive again.

Sunset

Dusk

Nothing more splendid than the setting of the sun
When the gleaming recedes and the dusk has begun;
Like an ancient drama choreographed in the skies,
He performs an endless role where he never dies—
Dancing in marvelous beams of crimson and gold
To a graceful bowing when night's curtains unrolled.

As a homeward traveler, the sun goes down to rest
In his brilliant abode of repose in the west;
As a thief who steals so greedily with his hands,
The darkness reaches out to the skies, through the lands;
As a silent witness, the earth would do nothing,
So the sun gets robbed by the night's dirty thieving.

Like the dark of night that comes inevitably,
In our lives would come some failures eventually;
All the light within us may completely be killed,
In the light of the dawn we'll completely be filled;
And the sun once again would rehearse through the day
To stage the only role he'll eternally play.

It is the
NIGHT
that reminds
us to live life
one day
at a time.

Darkest Night

We sometimes go through
the darkest night of our lives,
but then after that,
there's always
a morning.

Shine

I watched the moon
as she silently waltzes
across the star-studded
vast velvets of the night sky,
graceful among the glitters,
in the music unheard
but felt by the heart,
and as I watched her
gloriously glowing
without waiting
for any form of applause,
I began to realize
that just like the moon,
never would I need
anyone's approval
to shine.

Sometimes,
the moon
comes out by day
to remind us
that it is okay to
LOSE OUR GLOW
from time
to time.

Phases

Look at the moon.
    It is telling us
    that it is okay to go through phases.
You may sometimes lose your light
    but you will surely shine again.

Fret not
when life gets dark.
Always remember
that stars shine their
BRIGHTEST
in the darkest
nights.

How Lonely is the Moon?

On a clear evening sky or on a cloudy one,
As she hangs from the heavens through a string unseen,
Like a frolicking spider hanging from its web,
Do you take a pause to look at her and wonder—
How lonely is the moon?

Though the stars, her company, play with her,
And though how bright she outshines them all
As if jealous of the sun with all his brightness unsurpassable,
Do you take a pause to look at her and wonder—
How lonely is the moon?

When she shifts to her side for a quarter turn,
And shows us only half of herself
As if to imitate a model and flaunts with her curves,
Do you take a pause to look at her and wonder—
How lonely is the moon?

When she's not on the rise and the night is dark,
And the stars are left to sleep on their own
As if she shies away from the dark-demanding earth,
Do you take a pause to look at her and wonder—
How lonely is the moon?

At times when she decides to change her hue,
From white to ochre, and back again
As if she's bored of wearing the same veil,
Do you take a pause to look at her and wonder—
How lonely is the moon?

Even on a clear day when she chases the sun,
And takes their time together in the skies
As if she seeks to be gazed upon by an unfaithful lover,
Do you take a pause to look at her and wonder—
How lonely is the moon?

You are
like a star
that shines
BRIGHTER
when it's
dark.

Cold Night

Worry not about the cold
    and the darkness of the night
    for the golden sun shall always rise again
    and shine with the morning light.

Stars

The stars resemble the dreams
    we strive to reach day after day.
Though the clouds sometimes
    would block their twinkling,
    we still know that they are
    always there.

Every ending
is a prelude to
NEW BEGINNINGS.
Just as the night
makes way for
the sun to rise
again.

Counting the Hours

Sometimes,
counting the hours
before the sun appears
on the far horizon
makes the dawn seem longer
than it is.
Waiting can be hard, but in waiting,
there is hope.
And hope is the very thing
that makes us look forward
to a brighter day.

You may be in the darkest dawn
of your life right now, remember,
the sun will certainly rise.

Just be patient.

Wait and Hold On

No matter how long the night will be,
    behold, the morning will come
    for it doesn't have a choice.
All you have to do
    is wait and hold on.

You can
NEVER STOP
the night from coming;
but neither can you
stop the sun
from shining
again.

Here and Gone

They fall to the earth and disappear,
    the morning dew have known it since;
The stars that shoot across the inky skies
    have known how short is their sudden glory;
And just like them, we were born to grow,
    we stay for a while and we later go;
But there's not a thing that we should regret
    however short our stay may be:
We must live our fullest, our best, our all—
    for the life we have was given for free.